D0398968

This book was donated

to honor

the birthday of

Nick Levin

by

Sandra Muraak
~~David Levin~~

2003

Uses for Mooses,

And Other (Silly) Observations

Uses for Mooses,

And Other (Silly) Observations

BY

BILL SILLIKER JR.

Down East Books
Camden, Maine

ISBN 0-89272-484-6

Printed in China by Four Colour Imports, Ltd.

4   5

Down East Books
P.O. Box 679
Camden, ME 04843
BOOK ORDERS: 1-800-685-7962

Library of Congress Cataloging-in-Publication Data

Silliker, Bill, 1947–
        Uses for mooses, and other observations / by Bill Silliker, Jr.
            p. cm.
        ISBN 0-89272-484-6 (hc.)
        1. Moose—Pictorial works. 2. Moose—Humor. I. Title.

    QL737.U55 S5545 1999
    599.65'7'0222 21—dc21   99-044749

Contents

Introduction

    I Never Met a Moose I Didn't Like

Categories:

Dedication

It is really true that there's something about moose that makes me like them, no matter how large and ornery and scary some of them can be when we meet in the woods or on the open tundra or on a dark road at night. Moose really are special in some indefinable way.

And so this book is dedicated to all the moose I've ever known.

Introduction

I Never Met a Moose I Didn't Like

Moose hold a special place in the hearts of many people. I don't know just why that is. It may be that the moose represents wilderness. Perhaps moose are a symbol of simpler times and less hectic places.

Maybe it's also because even though they are large and strange looking beasts, moose have a mostly gentle demeanor. To borrow a phrase from Will Rogers, I never met a moose I didn't like. I have met a few that have scared me. But I never met one I didn't like.

Uses for Mooses, And Other (Silly) Observations, while presenting a less serious look at the species than my other works on moose, will still educate the reader a bit about moose behavior. Why? First of all, the moose all posed quite naturally for each of these photographs. I selected them from the tens of thousands of images in my files showing moose in mostly more traditional poses. And so, however odd some of these photographs might make moose appear, all are of normal, healthy moose just doing their thing.

The idea behind this book, though, is more to amuse than to educate. The captions evolved from a process of many inputs from several sources: a group of moose-photography enthusiasts on one of the Moose Getaway Weekends I led for L.L. Bean this year, the somewhat-less-than-sober comments of the 1999 attendees at my wife's annual "Cousin's Party," and the wit of selected friends.

We obviously took biological and poetic license. We attributed thoughts and, in some cases, speech to some of the moose. I can tell you that after having watched and photographed thousands of moose, I'm convinced that they actually do think. But, I've never heard one speak—except in moose talk. Don't you wonder what one might say if it could?

While some of our captions attribute to moose thoughts and behaviors that they do not exhibit, most actually reflect a grain of truth. Moose do demonstrate a great curiosity about the world around them. Moose do shed their coats and look rather ragged each spring. And moose do show tremendous athletic prowess. But care should be exercised in taking us too literally. For example, while bull moose often dance around each other during the fall mating season, I doubt that they call the step by the same name that we did.

And while one moose might chase another in what appears to be a game, moose "tag" is a very serious game, indeed. An angry or defensive moose might use its front legs to strike out in a manner similar to the behavior of a horse. A swift kick from a mad moose hurts and could even kill.

Any reader who thinks that we've made the moose on these pages appear more humorous than they do to each other is absolutely correct. In fact, I've never seen a moose laugh. But any reader who believes that we've treated this magnificent species unfairly should first ponder the question: What do you suppose a moose thinks when it looks at a human? Surely they must find us strange in appearance.

And what must go through a moose's mind when it watches a

human run away from it, or better yet, scramble gracelessly up a spruce tree? By the way, those escape techniques can be avoided if you develop a healthy respect for moose, as I have. That's not to say I haven't had to back away in a hurry when a defensive mother with a young calf—or a bull on the prowl during the fall mating season—decided that I was standing where it didn't want me to be.

And so, *Uses for Mooses, And Other (Silly) Observations* evolved. After much musing we divided the book into five chapters.

The opener delivers on the title and takes a look at a bunch of possible Uses for Mooses that I can guarantee you their Creator never considered, except perhaps for the one to do with bugs.

The next chapter, In the Minds of Mooses, seeks to explore moose thoughts about certain situations and to translate them into human speak.

Celebrity Mooses offers a moose version of some human figures, where either the moose's appearance or behavior reminds one of famous and, in some cases, infamous people.

Games Mooses Play shows what happens when a wildlife photographer has been in the woods with the mooses for too long. But I shot those photographs because the actions or the poses of the moose attracted my attention. Why? Because they looked funny to me at the time.

Which brings us to the last chapter of this whimsical work. Of Moose and Men puts it all together: funny poses by moose, thoughts one might read into their looks, and most especially, their interaction with humans—including one moose posing with a wildlife photographer who may have been in the woods with the mooses for too long (although I am the guy in the foreground—the farthest from the sleeping moose).

We hope that you enjoy this most mischievous look at moose. Should this book arouse your interest in seeing one of these fabulous creatures in the wild, I urge you to learn more about them before heading off to the big woods. Get your hands on my *Maine Moose Watcher's Guide* and my larger book on all four sub-species of the North American moose, *Moose: Giant of the Northern Forest.* Also available from Down East Books is the 45-minute VHS video I wrote the script for: *Maine's Magnificent Moose.* Armed with some knowledge you'll have a better chance to see and enjoy more moose. You'll also learn not only that there are many different uses for mooses, but also that the moose truly is one of the most magnificent animals alive today in our north woods.

Uses for Mooses

Uses for Mooses

My sincerest apologies to Mrs. Cory and Mrs. Moody and the other dedicated teachers who worked so hard to teach me the English language, but mooses just happens to rhyme better with uses than moose does. And since this chapter is all about the different uses one can find for a moose when one puts their mind to it, it only seemed natural to employ the incorrect plural form: mooses.

Consider the first image in this set. If you were the guy that just came out of the cabin to warm up for a hike and spotted those two hairy beasts in the yard, tell me you wouldn't be tempted to call inside to your buddies: "Hey, come take a look at the two mooses out here on the lawn."

Uses for mooses. See if you can't come up with some of your own that we didn't think of. Or perhaps we did, but we decided that the one here worked better. But it doesn't matter. Because only the moose know for sure.

1. Lawn ornaments

2. Moose crash dummies

3. A sure cure for
constipation

4. Moose security guard

5. Moose TV

6. Chocolate moose

7. Christmoose
tree trimmer

8. Hair transplant donor

9. Doorstop

10. Path finder

11. Ichthyologist (one who studies fish,
for those of you from Meddybemps)

12. To give bugs something to do

13. To give the tourists a thrill

14. Hedgehog imitation

15. Baby shower

16. Moose e-mail

17. To add flavor to pond water

In the Minds of Mooses

In the Minds of Mooses

Imagine for a moment that you could read a moose's mind. Consider what that moose might be thinking in any given situation.

Now imagine that the moose could speak in English. What might it say about the situation that it was thinking about? That's what we did as we assembled this chapter.

In fact, you can look at most of the photographs in this book and put words in the mouths of mooses. But since that seemed almost too easy, we limited our final selections for this chapter to those images that cried out for such moose speak. The caption developed by one of my friends at L.L. Bean is a perfect example: how could an image of a moose approaching a white sports utility vehicle—albeit not a Bronco—have any other caption?

18. "Do you think that the water tastes funny?"

19. "You're right—the water does taste a little funny."

20. "I sure could use a Bloody Mary."

21. "I wonder if she still has a headache."

22. "Kiss my pitootie!"

23. Sure proof that moose are nearsighted:
"O.J.? You in there?"

24. "I can get
MTV when I
turn
like this."

25. "Go ahead—make my day."

Celebrity Mooses:
The Famoose
and the
Infamoose

Celebrity Mooses:
The Famoose and the Infamoose

There is an old saw that goes that if you live with your dog long enough you wind up looking like it. Or is it the other way around? In any case, it's a fact that some moose remind you of people that you know.

That's where we started with this next chapter: mooses that looked like somebody famous. That evolved into covering mooses that exhibited behavior that reminded us of people from history.

Of course, we took a few liberties with history. But we could be close to right. I mean, can you name the guy that invented pizza?

My favorite is Moosa Lisa. Tell me that she's not beautiful with that smile.

26. Moosolini

27. Moosa Lisa

28. Cyrano de Bergerac stand-in

29. Dr. Timoosey Leary—
never could get through the woods without tripping.

30. Moosarella—the inventor of pizza

31. A Mafia moose pays his respects to the Don.

32. Who says there's no Bullwinkle?

33. Jimmy Durante wannabe

34. Wolfgang A. Moozart practices directing the orchestra

35. Sonny and Cher wannabes

36. Most people don't know that Chicken Little
was really a moose.

37. Zsa Zsa moose wannabe—
always powdering her nose

Games Mooses Play

Games Mooses Play

The words for this chapter came the easiest. Just look at each moose and tell me that you don't immediately see a connection to tag, peek-a-boo, or hide-and-seek.

And if you ever get the chance to watch mooses in the wild as they go about their day, you'll wonder that they're not playing games sometimes. Just remember that a moose plays to win.

38. Tag

39. Olympic high jumping

40. Touch football

41. Peek-a-boo

42. Hide-and-seek

43. Scratch and sniff

44. The do-si-do

45. The Charleston

46. Doubleheader

47. Water ballet

48. Hide-and-seek: the sequel

49. Chicken

Of Moose and Men

Of Moose and Men

Last but not least, this chapter includes photographs that show moose interacting with people. Moose are actually very curious animals, and they watch people much the same as we watch them.

Only in some cases, the people don't seem to notice the moose. Now I ask you: how could anyone miss an animal as large as a moose? And with the exception of the last photograph, none of these pictures was staged.

That last image, the one of myself and a friend sleeping with a moose, is not something you should try unless you really know the individual moose's behavior, and even then, you should keep a wary eye on the big fellow. Which reminds me of a final joke: Do you know where a moose sleeps?

Anywhere he wants.

May all of your uses for mooses be as much fun as the putting together of this book has been.

50. A moose-scat-ologist . . .
a moose that really knows his stuff.

51. Moose paparrazzi

52. Moose—watching
"And people say that we're dumb animals!"

53. Some moose know a photo opportunity
when they see one.

54. Presidential candidate—
all wet and full of bull

55. "Here she comes—Moose America."

56. Some people dance with wolves—
Bill Silliker sleeps with moose.

The
End